50 Deeds
for Those in Need

50 Deeds
for Those in Need

Andrew J. Nalian

WestBow
PRESS
A DIVISION OF THOMAS NELSON

WestBow Press books may be ordered through booksellers or by contacting:

WestBow Press
A Division of Thomas Nelson
1663 Liberty Drive
Bloomington, IN 47403
www.westbowpress.com
1-(866) 928-1240

ISBN: 978-1-4497-7904-7 (e)
ISBN: 978-1-4497-7905-4 (sc)
ISBN: 978-1-4497-7906-1 (hc)

Library of Congress Control Number: 2013900145

Printed in the United States of America

WestBow Press rev. date: 1/23/2013

Preface

My name is Andrew Nalian, and I am writing this book to make changes in my life, your life, and the lives of others around us.

I was born in Michigan, but during the year I wrote this book, I lived in Michigan, Alaska, and Vermont. While in Alaska, I was bullied pretty badly. I got a job there, but I was starting in the middle of the season. It was like being the person who replaced one of the roommates on the television program the *Real World.* I was an outcast.

One night, I was lying in bed and wondered, *How can I make this world a better place and win over my bullies?* A light came on in my mind, and I thought of a "good deeds" project. Every day, I looked up a motivational quote and tried to do at least one good deed for one of my bullies. I jotted them down on napkins or put them in my phone as notes to myself. I then decided to compile my good deeds into a book and challenge others to join me in my project by performing a good deed every day.

There are many people to thank for their part in creating this book, starting with my mother, Barbara, and my brothers, Tommy and Eric. As a family, we have been through so much, yet we have only grown stronger. You are my rocks, and I couldn't survive without all of you. I also give a special thanks to all of the friends I have met in my lifetime, be it my Phi Kappa Tau brothers, my friends in the Israeli Army, my 989 family, or anyone who has made eye contact with me and just smiled; you are the ones who help make the world a better place. I also must thank Rebecca Goldberg, who designed the cover of this book. You can find more of her work at www.rebeccamich.com. I also owe a big thanks to David Coleman. Without you, this book would not be anywhere near what it has become, and I truly thank you. Thanks to Paul Wesselman for all the advice you gave me during my process and helping me find out my true morals. Thanks also to Wendy Naarup for her insight and Eddie Boullion for his help on gathering a great story. Thank you to everyone who wrote a story for this book. I would also like to thank my publishing consultant, Donovan Gerken, as well as my check-in coordinator, Amanda Parsons. Last, I thank God, because without him, none of this would have happened.

20% of proceeds of all books sold will be donated to SeriousFun Children's Network. More than two decades ago, Paul Newman had a vision: imagine if children with serious illnesses had the chance to simply be children. To just have fun. So he started a camp where kids could, in his words, "raise a little hell." Today, Paul's legacy continues with SeriousFun Children's Network, a growing global community of independently managed and financed camps and partnership programs that create opportunities for children and their families to reach beyond serious illness and discover joy, confidence and a new world of possibilities—always free of charge.

My wish is that the wishes of those who are less fortunate than me can have their wishes come true.

—Andrew Nalian

Check this box
once you complete
the deed!

□ Chalk a
Motivational Message
on the Sidewalk

This book contains many inspiring quotes. Choose any of these quotes, and chalk it on the streets!

Go out of your way to help someone.

☐ Adopt a Soldier

Soldiers around the world are trying to save your life. What can you do for them? These individuals are just like you and I but are fighting for us to be free.

Some soldiers do not have anyone to write to. You can become a pen pal to one of these service members.

I recently met a group of soldiers from around the world and became great friends with them. I got each of their addresses so I can mail them a copy of this book.

*I like the dreams of the future better
than the history of the past.*
—Patrick Henry

☐ Buy a Reusable Shopping Bag

Paper or plastic?
Neither!

Do everything in your power to save the environment and the trees. Did you know that trees provide oxygen, improve air quality, help preserve soil, and support our wildlife? Think how dull the world would be without them!

In an underdeveloped country, don't drink the water. In a developed country, don't breathe the air."

—*Changing Times*

☐ *Donate Blood*

If you could save someone's life in exchange for enduring a brief needle prick and then get milk and cookies, would you? The Red Cross is always looking for blood donors. Every time you donate blood, it is like you are getting a mini physical, because your iron levels, blood pressure, and temperature are tested. This is a regular way to check your basic vitals and to make sure everything inside of you is working the way it is supposed to.

Just do it.
—Nike

▢ Scatter Good Luck

Go to a park or populated place and leave fifty pennies face-up as lucky pennies; my mother used to collect pennies left face-up for good luck. I once heard pennies are signs from angels. If an angel misses you, it will drop a penny to cheer you up. You can spread the luck and the cheer!

A penny saved is a penny earned.
—Benjamin Franklin

Couch to Contender

A Story by Michael Frederick

While changing my shoes at the gym, I saw a bright gold flyer on the table in front of me for a first time 5K training camp. *Do you know how far 5K is?* I was intrigued. This simple flyer changed everything for me.

In August of 2010, I had bariatric surgery for weight loss. At that time, I weighed 350 pounds and was noticing how increasingly difficult it was becoming to do simple daily things, like climb the stairs or walk long distances. I was drastically dropping the weight and wanted not only to lose the weight but to become radically healthier as well. I began working out at a local gym and doing some light cardio and upper-body strength training. I was primarily riding an exercise bike and walking on the treadmill for my cardio. Eventually, I got brave enough to try the elliptical and building some endurance. In late Janurary 2011, I saw that flyer. I began to wonder, *Is it even possible?* At the time, I couldn't even imagine running to the other end of the gym, but this concept of pushing myself to a goal of completing a 5K event (3.1 miles) intrigued me as much as it seemed impossible.

The class was still a few months out, but in my mind, I had already committed to joining. I intentionally went to the gym after work, around 3 a.m., so I could have the entire place to myself. I didn't want to embarrass myself on the treadmill as I began to attempt to run. I slowly increased the speed to a slight jog and began to smile. I couldn't run very fast or very far, but I was actually running. Each time on the treadmill, I increased my distance each time. I was up to a half mile and then I could do a mile without stopping. I was gradually building up ability and confidence.

A friend told me about a 5K in March. It was the Corktown 5K Race, which was held downtown just before the St. Patrick's Day parade. It was billed as a "no-pressure" run. I was even told there would be green beer at the finish line! So like anyone who had never run a race before would do, I jumped at the chance to register. I figured this would be a great test to see how far I could go in an event before attending the 5K training. Obviously, I would need to work harder at the gym. It wasn't until two days before the race that I finally was able to do 3.1 miles on the treadmill without stopping. Still, I had doubts about running outside for the first time.

The Corktown 5K Race was my first real test, and I was nervous and very cold. I watched my feet move underneath me in disbelief at times. I was one of thousands of people running that day, but at the same time, this was very personal. I kept a steady, even pace, and at the halfway point, I wanted to stop. When I made that turn to "come home," freezing rain was stinging my face, and fatigue was starting to set in. I told myself I had worked too hard and had already run too far to just give up. With that thought, I began to run faster, all the way to the finish line. I crossed that goal with tears in my eyes. I did it! I tell everyone the weight loss transformed me, but running has truly changed my life.

Since that first race, I have continued to push myself. I completed the 5K training camp as a way of paying respect to the one thing that motivated me to start in the first place. I began to do other 5Ks and 10K events. On August 14, 2011 (almost one year to the day of my surgery), I ran my first half marathon in Chicago; I weighed in at 198 pounds. I completed the 13.1 mile journey in two hours and fifteen minutes. I couldn't believe it. I was 350 pounds just one year before and struggled climbing up a flight of stairs to my car in the parking structure. I now participate in events that I had not been healthy enough to be a volunteer for just twelve months previously.

I have continued to push and challenge myself. I have run in about forty events since March of 2011, including seven half marathons, a one hundred-mile "century" bike ride for charity, an adventure triathlon, and my first full marathon. When we were babies, all we wanted was to take our first step. We should never let that drive and passion leave us. That first step, so long ago, has taught you everything you know today. Believe in yourself, because I believe in you.

There are only two mistakes one can make along the road to truth; not going all the way and not starting.

—Buddha

☐ Be a Role Model

Be aware of every action you make, for each sets the tone for the actions of everyone around you. Be someone you respect, and respect will come right back to you. Your character is built off the actions you do when no one is watching.

When I was coaching, the one thought
that I would try to get across to my
players was that everything I do each day,
everything I say, I must first think what
effect it will have on everyone concerned.

—Frank Layden

☐ Take a Picture
for Someone

I was getting into my car one day when I saw a family getting ready to take a picture. But the mother was not in it; she was taking the photo. People are shy, so take charge. Offer to take a photo that includes the whole family. A family picture should have the entire family in it.

A picture is worth a thousand words.

☐ Share Your Knowledge

If you're good at something, show it off in a helpful way. Go to your local library and offer to tutor someone in a subject you are good at. You may learn more than you think from helping others, and what a better way for you to stay keen on your knowledge as well!

A good teacher is like a candle; it consumes itself to light the way for others.

—Mustafa Kemal Atatürk,
translated from Turkish

❐ Support Local Businesses

People are trying to make a living doing what they love. Buy a local musician's CD. Go to a local restaurant, or shop at a locally owned store. Support your community. Supporting your local business helps create a better community well-being and keeps the hard-earned dollars in the local economy.

With all my fans, I got a family again.
—Tupac Shakur

☐ Write a Positive
Online Review

It is very easy to criticize something, but people are often hesitant to give compliments. If you had good service, tell everyone. If you liked a book, give it a five-star rating and a good online review. Share your passion. Share what you love. If you enjoyed something, let everyone know, so they can enjoy it, too!

On every thorn, delightful wisdom grows;
in every rill, a sweet instruction flows.
—Edward Young

☐ Start a Piggy Bank
for a Cause

You can take five cents a day—or all of your spare change—and throw it into a piggy bank. When the bank is full, donate the money to a charity. Research something you are passionate about and then find a charity that is passionate about it as well. Do your research; some charities use a larger percentage for good works than others. When you fill your piggy bank, donate it!

Just one penny can turn your thousands into a million.
—David Henkin

☐ Be Generous with Compliments

The smallest compliment can make a person's entire day. How many people's days do you feel like making today? When you are walking down the street, tell someone you like his or her shirt or outfit. If you went to a restaurant, tell your server he or she did a great job. Complimenting is easy. Try to do ten a day!

This above all: to thine own self be true.
—William Shakespeare

Give Him a Chance to Surprise You

A Story by Matt Glowacki

The actual day of my birth was a very special day for me of course, but it affected my parents in a way that would forever change their view of how to look at the world and what to expect from me. From what I understand, my mother's pregnancy with me was typical enough. It occurred during the early 1970s, and she didn't have access to the amazing baby-viewing technology common to most prenatal care facilities today. So the fact my legs did not develop was not apparent until my birth.

My father was in the supportive role in the hospital room with my mother as she was giving birth. Everything was going as planned. My father does recall the moment during the birth it was apparent his son was born without legs. The doctor's face and the mood in the room changed. My perplexed father asked about the nature of my defect, and it was reported I was normal except for the absence of my legs. In his mind, the vision of his life with my mother changed forever. They had just completed construction on their initial home, and it was a tri-level. With seven stairs between each floor, and now with a child with mobility impairment, he thought they would have to sell the home and make the first of many life changes that would paint a different picture of the future of his family.

He shared his revised plan with the doctor, including his belief they would have to sell the house. The doctor questioned him about the reason why, and my father explained the challenge of the stairs in the home. At that point, I believe my father received the best advice he could have ever heard. The doctor told him, "Don't sell the house. Why don't you give him a chance to surprise you." Little did he know, that change in expectation set up an entirely different way of looking at the challenges I would face for the rest of my life.

From that point forward, every perceived barrier became not an obstacle but an opportunity. It was our family's job to see what I could do, what I could accomplish. It wasn't always perfect. We went down a couple of incorrect roads because of the good intentions of others. But in the end, what mattered was meeting the challenges and learning from the experiences.

I learned how to traverse the stairs in our home, because my dad saw my ability to use my strength to pull my body up and down. All he needed to do was install the pull handles from a regular set of draws into the sides of the wall. I could grab the handles and negotiate myself up and down while doing a modified shoulder roll. As I got bigger and stronger, I could lift my body with my arms and balance my torso on each step. This provided me with the initial confidence to know if I had to get somewhere, I could do it by myself. I didn't have to rely on someone to take care of my most basic needs.

As I return to visit the house I grew up in, the handles on the sides of the stairs are gone, but the holes my dad drilled to hold them in place are still there. I see them every time I climb a stair on my hands today. They remind me of the love and vision my parents had for me and the effort they put into *not* doing the work for me, but establishing a way for me to do it myself. I was willing to try, and they were there to support me.

What I could do consisted of most of the things other kids my age could do. I was active in school, church, Boy Scouts, and many family events. However, when it came time for Little League or other advanced sporting activities, my family directed me to hobbies like stamp collecting and model trains. They were perfect for me. To this day, I have never felt that I missed out or had to settle for secondary experiences.

I have always appreciated working with my hands and making things. I would sit on chairs, the table, or the floor to construct my ideas. To this day, I find the floor to be the best surface for me to work on.

I had the chance to compete and excel against other people on a level playing field. The absence of legs really wasn't a factor because of the nature of those activities. I enjoyed myself and found I could attempt almost anything that didn't require legs. My disability was more of a factor in their mind than in mine. What they didn't understand was that any perception of disability didn't come into play in the activities I was participating in. I found myself excelling in areas where my wit and ability to share my ideas verbally allowed me an even playing field. I was all right as long as I didn't have to run fast or try to reach the top shelf. Eventually, and unbeknown to me, people started to see me as a leader and role model. They perceived me as having overcome a huge obstacle and capable of success.

I was never extraordinary; I was just me.

There is no better or bigger good deed a person can do for another person than assume they have the potential to be or do anything they set their mind to do, and then assist them in accomplishing those goals and realize their potential.

—Matt Glowacki

☐ Reach Your Potential

Reaching your potential truly isn't that difficult if you put your mind to it and believe in yourself. Start by reflecting on your life and being an optimist, not a pessimist, about your outcome. Then look up some role models who have done what you are trying to do, set your goal, be ready to learn, and embrace change. You may not get there the first time, but you will learn how to get there on your next effort.

Character is higher than intellect.
A great soul will be strong to live,
as well as strong to think.
—Ralph Waldo Emerson

☐ Don't Waste Food

For one day, don't waste any food or beverage. Be appreciative of what you have, because it is more than many others have.

If you have food in your fridge, clothes on your back, a roof over your head, and a place to sleep, you are richer than 75 percent of the people in the world.

If you have money in the bank, in your wallet, or some spare change, you are among the top 8 percent of the world's wealthy.

If you woke up this morning with more health than illness, you are more blessed than the million people who will not survive this week.

If you have never experienced the danger of battle, the agony of imprisonment, torture, or the horrible pangs of starvation, you are luckier than 500 million people who are alive and suffering.

If you can read this message, you are more fortunate than three billion people in the world who cannot read at all.

The rich would have to eat money if the poor did not provide food.
—Russian Proverb

☐ Stop Negative Conversation

During a negative conversation, there will be a point when you can join in—or stop it. Which route will you choose? Stopping negative conversations helps you become a much more positive person. If someone is complaining about the rain, remind them how much greener the grass will be in the morning.

Do what you can with what you have where you are.
—Theodore Roosevelt

☐ Bring in Your Neighbor's Trash Cans

If it's a windy day and you know your neighbors won't be home for a few hours, save them the grief of chasing their trash cans down the street. Take the trash cans up their driveways for them.

Each of us is a being in himself and a being in society, each of us needs to understand himself and understand others, take care of others, and be taken care of himself.

—Haniel Long

☐ Donate Old
Sports Equipment

A good friend of mine, Casey Smith, helped start something called Cleat Repeat. Cleat Repeat is a nonprofit organization dedicated to collecting new and used sports equipment and donating it to children in need. The organization aims to ensure all kids have an opportunity to participate in school and community athletics. Check out their Web site at www.cleatrepeat.org.

Don't bunt, aim out of the ball park.
—David Ogilvy

☐ Walk or Ride Your Bike

What is your carbon footprint? Leave the car at home for a day. Walking and riding your bike are both nonpolluting forms of transportation. You save money on your gas bill as well as help create a healthier you.

In America today, you can murder land for private profit. You can leave the corpse for all to see, and nobody calls the cops.

—Paul Brooks

Challenge Accepted

A Story by David Maiuri

My life changed in 1986. That's when my family was told their four-year-old boy's kidneys were failing. The doctors would soon diagnose me with focal segmental glomerulosclerosis, and within the next three years, I would need a kidney transplant to replace my native, infected kidneys or face dialysis and an uncertain future. Luckily, I was able to receive a kidney from my father in November of 1989 at University of Michigan Hospital. And despite some bumps in the road along the way, my life has turned out to be not so different from many others growing up in suburban Detroit.

Yet, I'm uncomfortable telling you that. Not because of the factual events of my life, not because it was a traumatic experience, and not because I'm living with a lifelong disease. It's because I'm uncomfortable using the words "change" and "different" to describe my story. After all, we're all different, and no two of us have lived the exact same lives. Sure, I encountered a medical condition that, thankfully, most never have to deal with, but who can say that one individual's experiences are more different or life-altering than anyone else's? We all face our own challenges and obstacles in the road every day. Why should mine be any more special?

Of course, that doesn't stop others from treating you differently. The hairless kid battling leukemia certainly gets some confused stares while walking down the hallway. The girl in a wheelchair will definitely be asked, "What's happened?" as she tries to get on an elevator. In my own case, teachers would often ask me what they needed to know about my condition should a situation come up. I was (and honestly still am) too proud to and nonchalant about my condition to offer anything, insisting that I am to be treated the same as everyone else. This is how we "sick" people want to be treated; like everybody else.

However, there is another, more important component to being sick: the mental component of what sick entails. There's really only two ways humans react to adversity: fight through the issue and refuse to let it stop them from achieving their goals, or let it encompass them, let it own them, and succumb to it. My only proof may be my firsthand knowledge of this, but I guarantee doctors would also tell you patients with a "let's beat this thing" attitude and an optimistic outlook are healthier than those who feel beaten and driven down by their condition. The latter group is not only sick in body but in spirit, too. These individuals often assume they cannot do certain things, like play sports, go out in public, exercise, or leave home for an extended period (whether short term for a vacation or long term for college). Perhaps most unfortunate of all, they pity themselves and expect pity from others. These people are their own personal defeaters.

Sorry, but either I wasn't raised like that, or I'm not built like that. Whatever it is, I don't consider myself sick at all. In fact, I probably only think about my condition ten or so times a year. My twice-daily pill routine? Just business as usual. Stepping out of the shower and seeing my abdomen, which is more carved up than most Halloween jack-o-lanterns? I hardly notice, and besides, it's been that way now for nearly twenty-five years. Getting my blood drawn once a month and sending it to my doctors at U of M hospital? A simple outpatient procedure that's not an inconvenience at all.

Not that there hasn't been attempts by others to use my condition to hold me back. I think the most obvious example was during my college years. When I first enrolled at Michigan State University in the fall of 2000, my health was in the midst of a steady decline. My first transplanted kidney was failing, as predicted by my doctors, as the changes my body went through during puberty slowly eroded the organ's effectiveness. By my sophomore year, I probably looked like one of the sickest people on campus. My body had very little energy at all times, and my skin had a pale, yellowish color. Students around the dorm constantly asked if I felt okay. And yet, I still made sure to make it to class as often as possible and to study regularly, as failing out was not an option in my mind. I wanted to graduate and do something with my life. Kidney disease certainly wasn't going to stop me!

By fall of junior year, my kidney function was down to about 20 percent, and I was at the point of needing another transplant. Of course, my body and my doctors were going to have to work around my schedule, as I was intent on finishing my first semester. In fact, my last final was scheduled for December 11, and I would have the transplant surgery (this kidney from my mother) on my first day of winter break, December 12, 2002. However, I found out my parents had planned for me to drop out of MSU for the following semester. They wanted me to attend local college "just in case" there were complications with the surgery or my condition. They pushed for me to stay local, and I pushed back to stay at MSU. Who were they to tell me what I could do regarding my education? Needless to say, my tenacity won out, and I returned to MSU the first day of the following semester.

Of course, being on a square-mile campus in the middle of a Michigan winter makes getting around tough for anyone, let alone somebody unable to move comfortably due to major surgery. Nothing a campus parking pass couldn't handle. And when parking lots near class were filled (as was often the case), I just parked a little further away and walked. Two feet of snow on the ground? I just got my boots on and left a little earlier than normal for class. Why would any of these "obstacles" stop me from graduation?

After four years at MSU, I graduated with a degree in finance and enjoy a successful commercial banking career today. In fact, I can honestly say that being an achiever with my disease has helped me spread the word about kidney disease awareness and, thus, been a benefit to my fundraising efforts with the National Kidney Foundation of Michigan, with whom I volunteer.

Although some may say I had a tougher childhood than most, my attitude has always been that everyone has their own challenges, but we can only play the cards life deals us. I know others have lived a much harder life than I, but why should I use my own life to make excuses? Some see obstacles; I see an opportunity to build character. Some say, "I can't." I ask, "Why can't you?"

Simply put, the only thing stopping us from achieving in life is ourselves. What better motivation does anyone need?

—David Maiuri

□ *Become an Organ Donor*

In the United States alone, hundreds of thousands of people are waiting for a donated organ. All it takes to save a life is a signature on a donor card.

> The gift that has been given to me says much about our capacity for great compassion and generosity, and I hope it sends an inspiring message to others about the importance of organ donation.
> —Steven Cojocaru

☐ Save Energy

Turn off lights and electronics when they are not in use. Join the global movement for energy conservation. This is the simplest way to join a cause; all you have to do is flick a switch. This will also help you save money, as well as reduce greenhouse gas, smog, and CO^2 emissions.

Conservation is a state of harmony between man and land.

—Aldo Loepold

□ Show Your Appreciation

Call a family member or a close friend and let that person know how you truly feel about him or her. People find it much easier to express negative feelings than positive ones, but why not spread a little cheer?

Never lose a chance of saying a kind word.
—William Makepeace Thackeray

☐ Donate a Book

People don't read enough today as it is, so I decided to donate the great book *How to Win Friends and Influence People* by Dale Carnegie. I gave this book to a dear friend, but you can donate yours anywhere. You can donate it to a public library, school, the Salvation Army, a church, or a friend. The possibilities are endless.

Wisdom passed along keeps the soul young.
—Allison August

□ Pick up Garbage

Leave every place cleaner than you found it, even if the litter is not yours. Try to devote one day a week to picking up all the litter you see. You will be astonished how much litter there truly is. Make an effort to keep your—and our—environment clean.

> What lies behind us and what
> lies before us are tiny matters
> compared to what lies within us.
> —Ralph Waldo Emerson

Forgive and Forget

A Story by Annette and Mike Castiglione

To forgive and forget is one of the lessons I was taught growing up in Catholic schools for twelve years. Those three words were simple and pretty easy to understand, or so I thought. On an October evening when my son Michael and I were settling in for the night, the phone rang and our lives were changed forever. My daughter, who was in her fourth year away at college, was fatally hit walking home from school.

Michael told me he listened that night to the conversation and wondered how bad her car was damaged. He never thought of the possibility he might never see his sister again. When reality set in, he wanted to know how the accident happened. Was the driver drunk? Was the driver speeding? It turned out the driver was distracted, because he was in the middle of an intense phone conversation. Michael became angry such an accident like this happened, one that could've easily been avoided.

After the funeral, life felt like a blur. An actual physical change took place in my body that was followed by anxiety and the panic that I did not know how to live without her. It is like everything you knew changed, and you had to learn all over again how to feel good, how to get out of bed each day, and how to want to be with others.

The next few months were very hard on Michael and me. Adjusting to life without his sister wasn't a smooth transition. Thanksgiving was a month after her accident, followed by Christmas and then her birthday in January. All those events were ones we would normally see and spend with her. As months turned into years, Michael was still angry and frustrated that the entire accident happened. He told me he couldn't help but constantly focus his anger on the driver of the car that hit her while she was walking across the street. When we talked about it, he said he didn't like how these negative thoughts toward someone were making him feel. It made him depressed and bitter. He would hide his emotions on the outside but didn't like the person he was becoming on the inside.

Michael was the main reason I put on the brave face and continued with the daily routines. I always taught my children that life is such a wonderful gift, but after this tragedy, I needed him to know that no matter what happened, we had to move on. I hid my tears from him as much as I could, so he would not see that I was barely holding on.

In time, the numbness started to fade. At times, I worried about how the driver who killed my daughter was doing, but my heart could not forgive him, even though

I knew it was the right thing to do. It was like I wasn't capable of forgiving and forgetting.

One night I turned on the television to get lost in some random program and take my mind off everything. I came across a program about Pope John Paul II. He had just passed away, so the station was running a special about him. He was seated in a prison, talking to a young man. For whatever reason, I could not change the channel. It was the man who tried to assassinate him years earlier. As I listened to the pope speak words of forgiveness, it was as if he was speaking to me. I felt an immediate healing in the deepest part of my heart, as if something was being pushed outside of me. I understood the meaning of forgiveness and felt it wash over me for the first time since my daughter's accident. I was so overwhelmed, I could not hold back the tears.

Michael started reading the Bible, and each time he opened to a random page, he said there was a message about forgiveness. He felt as if God was showing him how to forgive the driver of the car that took away his sister. He said it was like a weight had been lifted off of his shoulders as he found a way to forgive and forget.

Although life will never be the same for us, it is still so precious and wonderful. Michael and I have learned to love it as much as we had before. Looking back, I still don't understand how to forgive and forget, but I definitely have learned how to forgive ... from the bottom of my heart, with my whole heart, as I would want to be forgiven.

And whenever you stand praying, forgive,
if you have anything against anyone, so
that your father also who is in heaven
may forgive you of your trespasses.

—Mark 11:25

☐ Forgive Someone

Everyone makes mistakes. Think about a mistake you made. Remember how great it felt when you were forgiven without hesitation, because someone knew it was an accident? Now it's your turn; forgive someone without hesitation.

> You will know that forgiveness has begun when you recall those who hurt you and feel the power to wish them well.
>
> —Lewis B. Smedes

☐ Feed the Homeless

There was a homeless guy looking through my trash today, and instead of giving him money, I decided to buy him a meal. I know the meal will go to a good cause—feeding him—but I would have no way of knowing what the money would go toward if I didn't buy him the meal.

It is good to learn what to avoid by studying the misfortunes of others.
—Publius Syrius

☐ Treat Yourself

Some days you just need a break. Treat yourself to something—buy yourself some ice cream, go catch a movie, or put aside your work. Remember, you need to take care of yourself, too.

No matter what, there is always something to be thankful for.
—Andrew Nalian

Be Polite

Say please and thanks to everyone you see today. You will not believe the smiles you will get in response and the renewed energy you will feel from some kind words.

Let us be of good cheer, remembering that the misfortunes hardest to bear are those that never happen.

—James Russell Lowell

☐ Plant a Tree

This can be done in memory of a friend or family member or for no particular reason at all. If the tree is planted in memory of an individual, this tree can eventually watch over you. Remember all the good things trees can do for you.

Everywhere, man blames nature and fate, yet his fate is mostly but the echo of his character and passions, his mistakes and weaknesses.

—Democritus

The Boy Under the Tree

A Story by David Coleman and Kevin Randall

In the summer recess between freshman and sophomore years in college, I was invited to be an instructor at a highschool leadership camp hosted by a college in Michigan. I was already highly involved in most campus activities, and I jumped at the opportunity.

About an hour into the first day of camp, amid the frenzy of icebreakers and forced interactions, I first noticed the boy under the tree. He was small and skinny, and his obvious discomfort and shyness made him appear frail and fragile. Only fifty feet away, two hundred eager campers were bumping bodies, playing, joking and meeting each other, but the boy under the tree seemed to want to be anywhere other than where he was. The desperate loneliness he radiated almost stopped me from approaching him, but I remembered the instructions from the senior staff to stay alert for campers who might feel left out.

As I walked toward him, I said, "Hi, my name is Kevin,

and I'm one of the counselors. It's nice to meet you. How are you?" In a shaky, sheepish voice he reluctantly answered, "Okay, I guess." I calmly asked him if he wanted to join the activities and meet some new people. He quietly replied, "No, this is not really my thing."

I could sense that he was in a new world, that this whole experience was foreign to him. But I somehow knew it wouldn't be right to push him, either. He didn't need a pep talk; he needed a friend. After several silent moments, my first interaction with the boy under the tree was over.

At lunch the next day, I found myself leading camp songs at the top of my lungs for two hundred of my new friends. The campers eagerly participated. My gaze wandered over the mass of noise and movement and was caught by the image of the boy from under the tree, sitting alone, staring out the window. I nearly forgot the words to the song I was supposed to be leading. At my first opportunity, I tried again, with the same questions as before: "How are you doing? Are you okay?" To which he again replied, "Yeah, I'm all right. I just don't really get into this stuff." As I left the cafeteria, I realized this was going to take more time and effort than I had thought—if it was even possible to get through to him at all.

That evening at our nightly staff meeting, I made my concerns about him known. I explained to my fellow staff members my impression of him and asked them to pay special attention and spend time with him when they could.

The days I spend at camp each year fly by faster than any others I have known. Thus, before I knew it, midweek had dissolved into the final night of camp, and I was chaperoning the "last dance." The students were doing all they could to savor every last moment with their new "best friends"— friends they would probably never see again.

As I watched the campers share their parting moments, I suddenly saw what would be one of the most vivid memories of my life. The boy from under the tree, who had stared blankly out the kitchen window, was now a shiftless dancing wonder. He owned the dance floor as he and two girls proceeded to cut a rug. I watched as he shared meaningful, intimate time with people at whom he couldn't even look just days earlier. I couldn't believe it was the same person.

In October of my sophomore year, a latenight phone call pulled me away from my chemistry book. A softspoken, unfamiliar voice asked politely, "Is Kevin there?"

"You're talking to him. Who's this?"

"This is Tom Johnson's mom. Do you remember Tommy from leadership camp?"

The boy under the tree. How could I not remember?

"Yes, I do," I said. "He's a very nice young man. How is he?"

An abnormally long pause followed, then Mrs. Johnson said, "My Tommy was walking home from school this week when he was hit by a car and killed." Shocked, I offered my condolences.

"I just wanted to call you," she said, "because Tommy mentioned you so many times. I wanted you to know that he went back to school this fall with confidence. He made new friends. His grades went up. And he even went out on a few dates. I just wanted to thank you for making a difference for Tom. The last few months were the best few months of his life."

In that instant, I realized how easy it is to give a bit of yourself every day. You may never know how much each gesture may mean to someone else. I tell this story as often as I can, and when I do, I urge others to look out for their own "boy under the tree."

To the world you may be just one person, but to one person you may be the world.
—Brandi Snyder

☐ Make a New Friend

Don't be shy! What's the worst that can happen? The person you talk to will say no? Meeting new people will help you learn new things and better yourself. Look at what making a new friend did for Kevin and Tommy? It gave Tommy the confidence to tackle the world and to finally be himself.

Make your life a mission, not an intermission.
—Arnold H. Glasgow

☐ Volunteer at a
Nursing Home

So many individuals live at nursing homes with no family or friends to visit them. Ask someone at the front desk how you can participate in their volunteer program. You may have the opportunity to talk to a war veteran, a Holocaust survivor, someone who started their own business, or someone who set a world record! You will be surprised by the stories you will hear while visiting the elderly.

Your kind words and actions can save a life.
—Andrew Nalian

☐ Feed the Meter

Put money in someone's expired parking meter. The person may be in an interview that went longer than expected, taking a test, or doing anything! Returning to your car and finding a parking ticket is a real downer, so save someone's day by giving up some change. (This might not be legal in all states, so be careful!)

If you want to feel rich, count the things
you have that money can't buy.

—Proverb

☐ Donate Old Clothes

How many clothes do you have in your closet that you never wear anymore? Don't throw them out; donate them to the people in need. Goodwill, churches, and other organizations that run thrift shops are happy to take your donations.

Fear less, hope more, eat less, chew more, whine less, breathe more, talk less, say more, hate less, love more, and good things will be yours.
—Swedish Proverb

☐ Let Someone Cut in Line

Live life. Relax. If someone is in a hurry, let him or her go in front of you. Why would you want to rush through life? You only have one. I did a social experiment in New York City to see how many people would say thank you. You would be surprised at how this simple act can really warm up someone.

No man is an island.
—John Donne

☐ Leave Your
Change Behind

Have you ever been just a few cents short when paying for something? Why not leave your coins behind at a restaurant or store, so the next person who comes in will not have to worry about being short of change?

Believe that you have it, then you have it.
—Latin Proverb

☐ Smile at Everyone

Don't you love it when someone smiles at you? This little reminder shows people life isn't that bad. Look up, look out, look around you, and smile. A great way to build your confidence and self-esteem is to make eye contact with everyone you walk by and smile. If you are shy, this is a great way to start a connection with someone.

*A smile is an inexpensive way
to change your looks.*
—Charles Gordy

Title for the Unknown
(Antidote with no Anecdote)

Author Requests to Remain Anonymous

Being from the mitten state, Michigan, it is easy to show people where I live—I just point to my hand. When I was asked where I was born, the answer is not as simple. I was born in Feir, a small city in Albania. There was no stable government, with the communist government falling as Albania became an independent nation. After doing some research on where I came from, the story became frightening; I was an orphan in Vlora, Albania, living in a 1950s Russian army barrack run by US missionaries. The conditions were very rough but, fortunately, livable.

I was always afraid to tell people where I was from, feeling it revealed too much information about me. I also knew the questions that would arise. Do you know your parents? Did your parents keep it from you? Do you love your adopted parents? When these questions get asked, I am reminded of the biggest void I have in my life, not knowing my biological parents. My parents never hid the fact I was adopted, and I love them for that. But unfortunately, I do not know my biological parents.

I was adopted and came to the United States around the age of four. When I got here, I didn't know the language. My grandma on my new father's side was the one person I could communicate with the most. I spoke fluent Albanian, but my parents did not. My father told me a story about the first day he had to return to work. He told me how petrified my mother was to be left alone with me because of the language barrier between my mother and I. This is one of the many battles I faced and overcame.

I was on my way home from college for a weekend, and my uncle gave me a ride on his way back from up north. We started up the conversation about me being adopted. As we talked, the underlying subject was about my adopted parents. I have so much love for them and am thankful every day that they are my parents. He asked me where I thought I would be if I didn't have them. I told him bluntly I would either be dead or caught up in the wrong things. My adopted parents saved my life and fought for me. I ask myself every day what if I had missed that flight to my new home with them. When I see a plane in the sky, it means the world to me because that flight saved my life. I have no one other than my adopted parents to thank.

I am very honored to say I have come from being in an orphanage to becoming a college student at a big university. This is where I wonder, *Why me? How did I beat the odds?* The void of not knowing will always be there. As a kid, I didn't feel this void, but as I got older, it started to weigh on me. I wouldn't feel safe and no amount of music could calm me. After people found out I was adopted, they would ask questions. Each question was a reminder that I don't have a baby picture or that I don't know my blood ancestors. There was a point that the word "orphan" would make me choke up. The fact that there was no one I could talk to who could relate to me was hard, too.

I had no antidote to all the pain. I wonder if my biological parents think about me every day, like I think of them. I would get upset if people mentioned adoption. A few times things were said, that I would prefer not to repeat, and I would just die inside. I had to stop myself from bursting into tears. It was something I carried around that couldn't go away. I would get a feeling of being alone even when surrounded by loved ones. The one thing I miss the most is the truth. I miss my biological parents, and when I cry, no one can comfort me even. I feel alone and empty, and that's because those who try to comfort me are not my parents. I have come to the realization there is only one way to fill the emptiness. All I want is to hug my biological mother and father just once.

This is the first time I have ever written my story, and there is a puddle of tears on my keyboard from it. This is my turning point, the moment when my biggest fear helped me accomplish my biggest dream. My biggest fear is being completely alone, as an orphan would be. If you live through your greatest fear, what is left to fear? I began to realize that I lived as an orphan and lived through my greatest fear. When I was the most vulnerable, I had only feared myself. I will meet my biological parents one day, whether it is on this beautiful earth or when I reach those gates. This is when I realized the past will always be there, but I can't live there. I must live for the present and the future. I would rather stay up and make memories than sleep. I almost lost my life in the dangers of Albania when I was young, so now I must make every memory count. My biggest dream is to get my story out to the world, a story of inner struggle that healed. Don't be sad when you look at me. I now have that twinkle in my eye, because this is the first happy tear I have cried.

Always keep your head up. You never know
who is looking up to you for strength.
—Elliot Maksout

☐ Thank Your Parents

Or visit their grave. Let them know how they've inspired you. Let them know that if it weren't for them, you wouldn't even be here. Most of all, let them know you appreciate them. Take the previous story, for example. If this man was not adopted, who knows where he would have ended up. This is why he thanks his parents every day.

It kills you to see them grow up. But I guess it would kill you quicker if they didn't.
—Barbara Kingsolver

□ Thank Someone
in Uniform

Firefighters, police officers, and others in uniform risk their lives to save the lives of others. I believe they should be paid much more than any athlete or political figure out there. Express your appreciation for what they do.

I have spread my dreams beneath your feet.
Tread softly because you tread on my dreams.
—W. B. Yeats

☐ Help Someone Whose Car Has Broken Down

We see people pulled over on the side of the road all the time. Stop and see whether you can help. Maybe the driver's cell phone is dead, and they just need to make a call. Maybe she has a flat tire. Pull over, and ask if the person needs help. Even if you can't help, you will put the person in a much better mood just by being there.

Divide the fire and you will soon put it out.
—Greek Proverb

☐ Visit an Animal Shelter

Many schools have dogs visit the residence halls during exam weeks to help students relax. Why not relax yourself by making a visit to the animal shelter to pet or walk the animals? Dogs are always so excited to see us, and that translates into making us happier.

Lots of people talk to animals. Not very many listen, though. That's the problem.
—Benjamin Hoff

☐ Donate a Dollar

You can do this anywhere. Give a dollar to someone who is homeless, to an animal shelter, or to the little collection box by the register at a fast-food restaurant or grocery store. With credit cards and cell phones, it is easier than ever to donate. You've seen the commercials. Your one dollar could feed someone for an entire day.

Sometimes, when we are generous in small, barely detectable ways, it can change someone else's life forever.
—Margaret Cho

☐ Return a
Shopping Cart

Make someone's job easier, and return your cart to the store. What goes around comes around; maybe someone will make your work easier later on. I also know we all hate when carts are left in parking spots or get picked up by the wind and ding our cars.

Happy is the man who can do only one thing; in doing it, he fulfills his destiny.
—Joseph Joubert

☐ Make a Bird Feeder

The sounds of nature are wonderful, aren't they? Birds will also help your yard tremendously. Birds feed on seed, suet, and nectar as well as spiders and worms. Many small birds also love eating seeds from seed-bearing flowers and weeds, which can help eliminate weeds from your landscape!

How strange that Nature does not knock, and yet does not intrude.
—Emily Dickinson

Carey-ed by Angels

A Story by Carey Larabee

"Today I consider myself the luckiest man on the face of this earth." That was Lou Gehrig on July 4, 1939, when he made his famous farewell speech at Yankee Stadium. I am often reminded of this statement, because I am so fortunate to be surrounded by a great family and wonderful friends, who have made me the person I am today. Born with cerebral palsy, I use a power wheelchair and am faced with daily adversity.

I am very blessed in that I have two wonderful parents. Without them, I wouldn't be where I am. Since day one, they have supported and instilled in me not to let any obstacle get in the way of reaching my goals and dreams. They helped me realize that just because I may need assistance with daily living activities (i.e., transportation, dressing, showering) and do things differently than an able-bodied person, I can still have a successful life.

Born almost three months premature, doctors did not give me much of a chance to live because of a heart defect. In fact, I stopped breathing several times, but when I heard my mother's voice, I would open my eyes. She told the doctors I was a fighter and would survive, and like everything else, she was right.

At two weeks old, I was transferred from Wayne County Hospital in Detroit to the University of Michigan to have open-heart surgery. (I truly believe this is the reason I bleed maize and blue!) It wasn't until I was a year old, however, that my parents learned I had cerebral palsy, which affected my central nervous system as a result of a lack of oxygen at birth.

By age thirty-two, I have had twenty-four major surgeries and endured countless hours of physical and occupational therapy. Would I change a thing? Absolutely not! This journey has made me stronger and helped develop me into who I am. Though I will never forget the day I fully realized I had a disability.

My mom asked me that age-old question, "What do you want to do when you grow up?"

My answer was simple: "Play second base for the Detroit Tigers!

She explained to me that due to my disability, I wouldn't be able to play. Not to disappoint, she quickly told me there were other ways to be involved in sports. Sports have always been a huge part of my life, a vehicle and extra motivator to help me overcome adversity.

In 1984, shortly after the Tigers captured their fourth World Series title, I had the privilege of spending the day with legendary broadcaster, Ernie Harwell. At the time, I did not fully understand the role of a broadcaster. I simply knew that Ernie attended each Tiger game and was paid to talk about it! But from that day forward, my goal was to be a play-by-play broadcaster.

My dad has always stressed the importance of setting goals. In order to become a broadcaster, I had to graduate from college. For me, that was an easy choice. I set my sights on a degree from the University of Michigan! I knew it wouldn't be easy, and there would be a quite a few bumps along the way.

Despite my preschool teacher's belief I would never learn to read or write, I graduated high school as class valedictorian. I give much of the credit for my success to parents. During my elementary school years, my mom fought with our local school system just so I could attend school close to home. I had to travel two hours each way on the bus to another school district, because I was classified by the state as a "special ed" student, despite being enrolled in regular education classes. When I was finally admitted into the local district, my grades soared, and I never looked back. As I went through middle and high school, my dad spent hours with me, critiquing my papers and homework. Outside of the classroom, I spent a lot of time broadcasting my school's football and basketball games. My hard work paid off, and my dream came true. I was accepted and officially became a Michigan Wolverine!

Prior to my enrollment to the University of Michigan in 1998, I completed an intense, two-week physical and occupational therapy program at C. S. Mott Children's Hospital. As my rehabilitation progressed, there were times I became tired, needed energy, and just wanted to go home.

However, that was until I received a special visit from some U of M student-athletes. Then my demeanor changed. For a sports enthusiast like myself, I could not have been more thrilled!

Noting my excitement, From the Heart codirector Ed Boullion asked if I would like to volunteer once I became a student. He provided me with a wonderful opportunity, considering others have introduced me to many of my favorite athletes all my life. From then on, I had a chance to give something back by accompanying a group of student-athletes to the hospital on a weekly basis.

To see a child smile when he or she is introduced to a Michigan student-athlete brings a special feeling. The satisfaction I received knowing I helped make someone's day is more gratifying than any visit I have ever received. Helping these courageous children forget about being hospitalized is what From the Heart is all about, and it is truly a pleasure to contribute to its cause. In addition to the sense of pride it has given me, Michigan from the Heart has shown me the way to keep life in perspective by teaching a most valuable lesson: to always be thankful for what I have.

I will forever cherish my years at U of M. Not only did I broadcast Michigan women's basketball on campus TV, my involvement with From the Heart introduced me to a new aspect of sports: community relations. In 2003, I completed an internship with the Detroit Tigers and then worked with the Ann Arbor Center for Independent Living, developing sports and recreation programs for people with disabilities.

Now living in Orlando, I work at ESPN Wide World of Sports (EWWS), where I still have an opportunity to make kids smile and help their sports dreams come true. While at EWWS, I have been fortunate to be a part of some special events, including Atlanta Braves spring training and Tampa Bay Buccaneers training camp. As a guest operations cast member (Disney lingo for employee), the most enjoyable aspect of my job is assisting our guests with disabilities. Whether it's giving them a behind the scenes stadium tour or helping them get an autograph from a favorite player, I love to bring the game to life.

People frequently ask me if I have ever dreamed about playing sports. While I would be lying if I said I had not thought about throwing a touchdown pass or hitting a game-winning home run, I have experienced aspects of sports most people can only dream about. Kissing the Stanley Cup, carrying the Olympic torch en route to Salt Lake City, and attending Super Bowl XLI are special moments I will hold close to my heart forever.

At the end of the day, my triumphs in life are not all about me. Sports and life are very similar in that we are only as a good as the people around us. From Algonac (where I grew up) to Orlando, I have always been surrounded by great people who have been instrumental to my success.

It is often said that fortune is measured by friendship. I am living proof that Lou Gehrig was not alone in his comments.

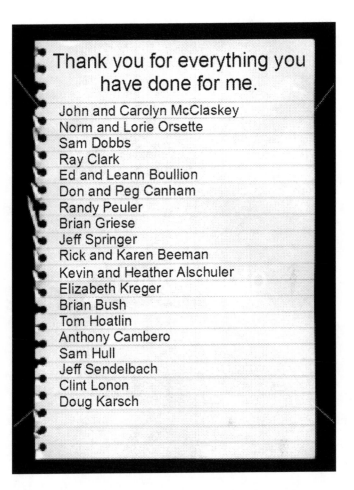

Thank you for everything you have done for me.

John and Carolyn McClaskey
Norm and Lorie Orsette
Sam Dobbs
Ray Clark
Ed and Leann Boullion
Don and Peg Canham
Randy Peuler
Brian Griese
Jeff Springer
Rick and Karen Beeman
Kevin and Heather Alschuler
Elizabeth Kreger
Brian Bush
Tom Hoatlin
Anthony Cambero
Sam Hull
Jeff Sendelbach
Clint Lonon
Doug Karsch

Some people are always grumbling because roses have thorns; I am thankful that thorns have roses.

—Alphonse Karr

☐ Express Your Gratitude

Write a letter to someone who's made a difference in your life. It can be a family member, friend, coach, priest, rabbi, Santa, or a teacher. Just let the person know! Your kind words will spread much more joy than you can imagine.

Without inner peace, it is impossible to have world peace.
—His Holiness, the Dalai Lama

☐ Hold the Door
for Someone

People tend to rush. If they see someone walking too slowly, they will not hold the door open. But maybe the person walking slowly cannot walk any faster. I can guarantee that person will appreciate the extra few seconds you waited to hold the door open.

Follow until you are lost, then lead.
—Ryan Wallis

☐ Pick up Your Friend's Tab

A good friend of mine was a victim of identity theft. He was very short on money. We all wanted to go out, but he had no money to spend, so I covered him. He had a good night out with his friends. That friend, Bob Simmons, is now creating art for me with quotes from this book. You can find his art at www.50DeedsForThoseInNeed.com.

Sometimes, it's the smallest decision that can change your life forever.
—Keri Russell

☐ Donate to a Food Pantry

How many times have you looked in your refrigerator and said, *Where is all the food?* In reality, you may have an excess amount of food, just none that suits your current taste. Imagine what it would be like if you opened your cabinet and there was no food at all? If you have excess food, donate it to your nearest pantry.

> He who obtains has little. He
> who scatters has much.
>
> —Lao-Tzu

☐ Give Someone a
Ripples Card

Paul Wesselmann started a great project called the Ripples Project. Paul is a motivational speaker who hands out "ripples cards" with motivational quotes on them. His idea is for those cards to be given as gifts and shared with friends, family, and even strangers. You can hide them for other people to find or do whatever you'd like with them. The choice is yours. Paul was kind enough to let me create my own ripples cards, which you can print online for free at www.50DeedsForThoseInNeed. com.

Limitations live only in our minds. But if we use our imaginations, our possibilities become limitless.
—Jamie Paolinetti

☐ Have a Charity Day

Suggest a charity day at work or school. Have your coworkers or classmates bring items they do not want anymore and hold a silent auction. Do this once a month. Let the person who organizes it pick the charity you'll donate the money to.

To your enemy, forgiveness. To an opponent, tolerance. To a friend, your heart. To a customer, service. To all, charity. To every child, a good example. To yourself, respect.
—Oren Arnold

I Grew up in Hiding

A Story by Arnie Sleutelberg

Both of my parents survived the Holocaust, my father by leaving Holland just in time, my mother, as a hidden child in the attic of a farmhouse for two years and seven months. My father had settled in a small Michigan town in 1940 with his parents and brother. They chose Hudson, in part, because there were no other Jews. There they could attempt to blend in by not revealing their Jewish background. By the time my mother joined the Sleutelberg family and my sister and I were born, the culture of hiding was firmly established. We grew up with strict instructions to never reveal our identity. We were to change the subject or say nothing if it came up. By the time I was in the fifth grade, my parents felt safe enough to have our names on a Jewish list and joined the temple in Jackson, thirty-five miles away. But they were not yet comfortable enough to share even my bar mitzvah two years later with any of our Hudson friends or associates. None were invited.

In retrospect, the whole thing was an illusion. Everyone knew we were Jewish, but we could delude ourselves into thinking they did not know by never talking about it. Only when I was in high school did we begin to acknowledge who we were. Then, in my senior year, the Hudson Tigers Marching Band accepted an invitation to march in the Salute to Israel parade in Manhattan. For the year preceding our trip, the Israeli flag was carried next to the US flag in the color guard while I, on my trumpet, and the rest of the band marched the streets of Hudson and on the football field playing "Hava Nagila."

The trip to New York in May 1976 was eye-opening for us all, especially for me. It was the first time I had experienced the world of Jews. As the lead band, we came to a halt in front of the viewing stand for the opening ceremonies. There were speeches followed by the singing of Israel's nation anthem, "HaTikvah." As it began, I felt the 150 pairs of eyes of the entire band look at me, while I, embarrassed, revealed with my red face that I didn't know the words. In that moment, I vowed to learn what it means to be a Jew.

I didn't know at that time, nor even for five more years, that I would become a rabbi. But after much learning and active engagement with Judaism, it seemed like the only appropriate profession for me. No more hiding being Jewish.

But a different kind of hiding began. It's called being in the closet.

While I had known since age seven or eight that I was gay, I didn't know what that meant. I assumed it would change. It didn't. But I had become so good at hiding my Jewish identity, it was easy to hide being gay too. The difficulty of the closet didn't emerge until college and seminary. Every year of hiding took its toll. I was suffocating in the closet. I had tortured myself by thinking my life would be over and that I would have to start anew. I finally came out at age twenty-seven, but only because there was no way I could stay in the closet even one more day. Though my fear of losing everything and everyone I held dear kept me in the closet for decades, there came the time when I had no choice but to be me and acknowledge my sexual orientation.

Fortunately, my fears were baseless, and everyone in my life accepted me as a gay man. My mother, of blessed memory, said after my revelation, "I still expect that he be Jewish."

Fast-forward twenty-five years.

I've been serving the same congregation since my ordination twenty-five years ago. Shir Tikvah has a year of anniversary celebrations planned. Plus, I just married my husband at ceremonies in Canada, England, and here in Michigan, with more than six hundred family, friends, and congregants in attendance, all effusively celebrating our love and commitment to each other.

If only I had had my current level of faith in the goodness and kindness of humanity thirty-five years ago, when I was struggling with coming out. But, I guess, growing up knowing most of my family were murdered just for being who they were, did not nurture that faith within me. Now, however, with abundant faith, I live openly and vibrantly in the fullness of who I am. My life is richly blessed.

To be yourself in a world that is constantly
trying to make you something else
is the greatest accomplishment.

—Ralph Waldo Emerson

☐ Be Yourself

There is no reason for you to be anyone but you. There is no better feeling than being loved for who you are, and no worse feeling for being hated for who you're not. Don't hide your quirks and rid yourself of your insecurities. Be who you are meant to be, and others will be greatly attracted to you. You don't want to live your life in hiding.

Be Yourself; everyone else is already taken.
—Oscar Wilde

❏ Create Your Own Deed and Quote, and Submit a Story!

Do you want to be in our next book? Did you love the deeds that you read but think you can create your own? Did you like the stories and think your story can have a strong impact on readers as well?

If so, I would love to hear them! You can upload all of these at www.50DeedsForThoseInNeed.com as well as e-mail me at TheDeedDoctor@gmail.com. For your deed, you can upload a picture, a video, or write out what you have done. For your story, you can type it, send me pictures, or make a video. Just think, you can be in our next book!

And in the end, it's not the years in your life that count. It's the life in your years.
—Abraham Lincoln